I Give Thanks: 30 Days of Prayers

Julian Marie Walker

"But if anyone loves God [with awe filled reverence, obedience, and gratitude], he is known by Him [as His very own and is greatly loved]" (1 Corinthians 8:3).

Amen.

ISBN: 978-1-956884-29-6

Contributing Editor: All services completed by Imprint Productions, Inc.

Cover Design: All services completed by Imprint Productions, Inc.

Printed in the United States of America Published by Imprint Productions, Inc.

Hello, Dear Reader,

Thank you in advance for purchasing this prayer book.

This book is a living anointing and testimony of the Holy Spirit of Jesus Christ. It was difficult to complete because of life's trials and the loss of love, which caused a delay in its delivery. Nevertheless, it was worth the wait.

Subsequently, I can personally tell you how great and powerful God is and the miracles He works through prayer. This is a true faith book. It is the edification and manifestation of powerful prayers and wonders.

Read and use every prayer with expectation. Be open to many blessings.

In Jesus Christ's mighty name, Amen.

Table of Contents

1. Gracious Father

Our Father, you are good and gracious to your children. "The LORD is gracious and full of compassion, slow to anger, and great in mercy" (Psalm 145:8). We honor you, LORD ALMIGHTY. We worship you because you are the Alpha and the Omega, the first and the last, therefore our forevermore. We trust that whatever you, our Father Lord Jesus, start, you are faithful and will finish it to the end. Thank you for being in our presence and giving us amazing love.

Thank you for being here with us. Thank you for loving us on Mount Everest and across the Atlantic Ocean. Thank you for carrying us through the rough times to a clear and prosperous path. According to Revelation 1:8, "I am the Alpha and the Omega," says the Lord God, "who is, and who was, and who is to come, the Almighty." Thank you for being our truth, our faith, our hope, and our dreams.

Thank you for keeping us wise, healthy, and forever young. May you, LORD, continue to shine your grace on us. According to Numbers 6:25, "The Lord make his face shine upon thee, and be gracious unto thee." LORD, we are grateful. In Jesus' name, we pray.

Ameen.

Dear reader!

Today, we take our faith to a higher level in Jesus Christ, regarding your family, health, and finances. Therefore, for every good and pure thing you believe in God for, you can join the Spiritual Agreement page. Write down your request and sign it!

____

____

Sign ____

We the body of believers ask God for supernatural miracles and manifestations according to his word John 14:14, " If ye shall ask anything in my name, I will do it". Thank you, Lord Jesus, in advance for your care and abundant good blessing in the Mighty name of Jesus!

Amen.

Sincerely, Julian Marie Walker

Author/Intercessor/Missionary

2. Requests be made known unto God

Holy, holy, holy God Almighty, we give glory to your holy name.
Father God, we come before your presence with thanksgiving and
praise. Father, we have seen your wonderful works and the answers
to our petitions in prayer granted. Lord God Almighty, when we turn
to you, we know that there is nothing you cannot do. We put all our
hope in you, Lord, and you faithfully listen to our requests and grant
us remarkable favors.

According to your Word in Philippians 4:6, "Fret not about
anything, but in everything, by prayer and supplication with
thanksgiving, let your requests be made known unto God." And in
verse 7, "And the peace of God, which passeth all understanding, shall
keep your hearts and minds through Christ Jesus." Great are you,
LORD. We honor you for who you are and blessed is your name. We
give thanks on this day!

We are joyful in spirit, soul, mind, and body. The joy of the Lord is
our strength, and glory and honor belong to you. Our Father, we come
to you in the name of Jesus Christ, our Lord and Savior, asking, if it is
your will, that we may have an abundance of love, faith, kindness,
happiness, hope, good health, grace, guidance, mercy, righteousness,
patience, passion, peace, power, protection, understanding, wealth and
riches, wisdom, knowledge, salvation, freedom, and financial stability
in Jesus' holy and righteous name.

Father, we thank you in advance. May you, LORD, add a bountiful
blessing to our request in the name of the Father God, His Son Jesus
Christ, and the Holy Spirit

Dear reader!

Today, we take our faith to a higher level in Jesus Christ, regarding your family, health, and finances. Therefore, for every good and pure thing you believe in God for, you can join the Spiritual Agreement page. Write down your request and sign it!

____

____

Sign ____

We the body of believers ask God for supernatural miracles and manifestations according to his word John 14:14, " If ye shall ask anything in my name, I will do it". Thank you, Lord Jesus, in advance for your care and abundant good blessing in the Mighty name of Jesus!

Amen.

Sincerely, Julian Marie Walker

Author/Intercessor/Missionar

3. O Lord, my strength

Most great and glorious Father God, I first give you thanks for life, health, and strength. Accordingly, "I will love thee, O Lord, my strength" (Psalm 18:1). Thank you for keeping me, my family, and my loved ones strong in faith. The joy of the LORD is my strength and my redeemer. Father God, may we approach your throne this day to give honor and praise unto you.

When we were weak, you carried us. When we are sick, you heal us in body, mind, and spirit. When we lose hope, you give it back to us. LORD, when we are low in faith, you increase it. When we mourned, you comforted us. When we were lost, you found us and redeemed us. When we asked for the sun, it shone brightly. When we asked for the rain, you sent it abundantly. When we are hungry, you feed us manna from heaven. When we were thirsty, you gave us water.

When we needed oil, you told us to gather our vessels. When we are sad, you send joy in the morning. When we need protection, you appear, Most High God, and block all gates of earth and hell. When we need care, Father God, you show up with your tender mercies every day. When we needed love, you provided the best for us. When we needed shelter, you gave us a home. What is impossible for man is not impossible for you.

There is nothing that you cannot do, so today we boldly boast and tell the world that we have a great Father. "He said to me, 'My grace is sufficient for you, for My strength is made perfect in weakness.' Therefore, most gladly I will rather boast in my infirmities, that the power of Christ may rest upon me" (2 Corinthians 12:9). We declare that our God can do all things. In our weakness, God's strength, power, and grace are given to us freely with love and guidance.

He can do all things for us as long as we ask. We declare and decree God's Word: "The LORD is my strength and song, and He has become my salvation; He is my God, and I will praise Him; my father's God, and I will exalt Him" (Exodus 15:2). We give thanks in advance for His great love and strength in the name of the Father, His Son Jesus Christ, and the Holy Ghost Spirit, I pray.

Amen and Amen.

Dear reader!

Today, we take our faith to a higher level in Jesus Christ, regarding your family, health, and finances. Therefore, for every good and pure thing you believe in God for, you can join the Spiritual Agreement page. Write down your request and sign it!

____

____

Sign ____

We the body of believers ask God for supernatural miracles and manifestations according to his word John 14:14, " If ye shall ask anything in my name, I will do it". Thank you, Lord Jesus, in advance for your care and abundant good blessing in the Mighty name of Jesus!

Amen.

Sincerely, Julian Marie Walker

Author/Intercessor/Missionar

4. Father of Justice bless your Righteous People

Father of Justice I come to you this day with hopes that you God define Justice that is righteousness greater than the law of this land and Nation. "Blessed are they who observe justice, who do righteousness at all times" (Psalm 106:3). Father, you promised your people hope, love, and peace with a Godly inheritance and by faith we received.

Accordingly, you Lord said, "But let justice roll down like waters, and righteousness like an ever-flowing stream" (Amos 5:24). First and foremost, Lord we seek ye first the Kingdom of God and recognize that you God are one true living God on earth and heaven. LORD of Harvest it is through faith that we receive your Godly blessing. Father God, we accept our rightful place on this earth, as your believer that we are the lawful heir to all good and great blessings.

Father, God Almighty, You Great and Mighty God, now release your full power and blessing that was held up in the Heaven spiritual rim for me. Therefore, throughout all the earth from east to west, north to south with the powers of the Holy Spirit, God our Father, and his son Jesus Christ we received joyful and divine blessings from the Lord. We received God's bountiful and rich blessings. "The heavens declare his righteousness, for God himself is judge!" (Psalms 50:6).

Father, we thank you, our covenant-keeping God, wonder working God. Lord of my life and salvation I pray for all glory; praise and honor is yours. Hallelujah, my God is faithful and Awesome in all his ways. He is powerful and great therefore we pray for righteousness and Justice for you people. "To do righteousness and justice is more acceptable to the Lord than sacrifice" (Proverb 21:3).

I decree and declare that my God is love and if he said it is so. We pray for our children this day that they may also be heir to the kingdom of God. Therefore, undeniable "Taste and see that the Lord is good; blessed is the one who takes refuge in him" (Psalms 34:8).

In Jesus' name, we pray Amen.

Dear reader!

Today, we take our faith to a higher level in Jesus Christ, regarding your family, health, and finances. Therefore, for every good and pure thing you believe in God for, you can join the Spiritual Agreement page. Write down your request and sign it!

____

____

Sign ____

We the body of believers ask God for supernatural miracles and manifestations according to his word John 14:14, " If ye shall ask anything in my name, I will do it". Thank you, Lord Jesus, in advance for your care and abundant good blessing in the Mighty name of Jesus!

Amen.

Sincerely, Julian Marie Walker

Author/Intercessor/Missionary

5. Where the Spirit of the Lord is, there is freedom

Abba Father, my great and mighty God, hear my prayer and attend to my request, O Lord, whose heart is heaven. Lord, I give thanks and praise, as so many of my generation have before me. It is with a clean heart and lifted hands. "Let my prayer be set forth before you as incense, and the lifting of my hands as the evening sacrifice" (Psalm 141:2). On bended knees, I come to you, Lord, in prayer. "Thus, will I bless thee while I live: I will lift up my hands in thy name" (Psalm 63:4).

Heavenly Father, I am giving you the best of me with all that I have and all that I am. Father, I choose to honor and praise you, thanking you fully, knowing that I am worshiping you always in the Holy Spirit with which you have anointed me from birth. According to 2 Corinthians 3:17, "Now the Lord is the Spirit, and where the Spirit of the Lord is, there is freedom." Father, thank you for granting repentance. Thank you for your redemption.

Ephesians 1:3 says, "Blessed be the God and Father of our Lord Jesus Christ, who has blessed us with every spiritual blessing in the heavenly places in Christ." Father God, I thank you most for salvation and the divine gift of daily renewal and restoration of my faith, hope, love, health, and wealth. Father, I pray for my loved ones. Please see to it that they also have the best of you, as I do. I thank you, as always, with great confidence that you take care of all matters concerning me.

How could I not love you? I love you because you loved me first. Thank you wholeheartedly. In Jesus' matchless name I pray. May the Lord add a blessing to this prayer forevermore.

Amen and Amen.

Dear reader!

Today, we take our faith to a higher level in Jesus Christ, regarding your family, health, and finances. Therefore, for every good and pure thing you believe in God for, you can join the Spiritual Agreement page. Write down your request and sign it!

____

____

Sign ____

We the body of believers ask God for supernatural miracles and manifestations according to his word John 14:14, " If ye shall ask anything in my name, I will do it". Thank you, Lord Jesus, in advance for your care and abundant good blessing in the Mighty name of Jesus!

Amen.

Sincerely, Julian Marie Walker

Author/Intercessor/Missionary

6. EL Elyon is Jehovah

Heavenly Father, thank you. You still amaze me daily.
Father, your divine grace covers me day and night. My daughter
frequently asks me what I would do without you, Mommy. Well,
Lord, out of the mouths of our children, what would I do without
you? Thank you for your love, grace, and continued mercy day
after day. Lord, I am not just saying this to appease you. I
sincerely mean it. Father God, sometimes it gets emotionally
hard to find out that the people we trusted are dishonest and not
worthy of our trust.

Lord, I know I am not perfect, and that the only person in this
world who holds that title is you, O Lord.

So, this morning, I'm going to step in line with faith and say
thank you for carrying me when I could not walk. Thank you for
being my eyes when I could not see. Thank you for my hands
and feet. Thank you, Lord, for being my strength daily and
continuing to work in divine purpose through me. Lord, thank
you for my pure and righteous thoughts. The Bible states that
whatever things are pure are where my thoughts should be.
Philippians 4:8 says, "Finally, brethren, whatsoever things are
true, whatsoever things are honest, whatsoever things being just,
whatsoever things are pure, whatsoever things are lovely,
whatsoever things are of good report; if there be any virtue, and
if there be any praise, think on these things."

Father God, accordingly, I praise you and leave those things and that life behind me, looking only unto you for all that is virtuous and clean. I give thanks that I have a blessed life despite all obstacles. How does that song go? "I tasted and saw the sweetest of love," but nothing can compare to you, Lord. Blessed is your name, and great are you, Lord. I'm most thankful for my children and grandchildren and for having the blessing of a good woman as a mother. Lord and most gracious Father, let me take this moment to forgive myself and others.

Lord, if I was introverted or accidentally did or said anything to harm or hurt anyone, forgive me, because you know that was never my intention. I was never raised like that or to cause anyone pain. I come boldly in the Spirit, casting out illness, hurt, and poverty in Jesus' name. The Bible states in Joshua 24:15, "And if it seems evil unto you to serve the LORD, choose you this day whom ye will serve, whether the gods which your fathers served that were on the other side of the river, or the gods of the Amorites in whose land ye dwell. But as for me and my house, we will serve the LORD."

Lord, you know I declare, "But as for me and my house, we will serve the Lord," and this covenant will be for eternity for me, my children, and every offspring and lineage after me.

Father, thank you, El Elyon, my Most High God. My Yahweh, my Lord Jehovah, thank you for being Jehovah Raah, my Lord, my Shepherd. Jehovah Nissi, Lord my Banner. My

Jehovah Rapha, my Lord who heals. Jehovah Shalom, my Peace. My Jehovah Jireh, my Lord who provides. Jehovah Shammah, Lord who is there. Thank you for being Adonai, my Lord and Master. Lord, you declare in your Word, "I am Jehovah, that is my name; and my glory will I not give to another, neither my praise to graven images" (Isaiah 42:8).

Dear reader!

Today, we take our faith to a higher level in Jesus Christ, regarding your family, health, and finances. Therefore, for every good and pure thing you believe in God for, you can join the Spiritual Agreement page. Write down your request and sign it!

____

____

Sign ____

We the body of believers ask God for supernatural miracles and manifestations according to his word John 14:14, " If ye shall ask anything in my name, I will do it". Thank you, Lord Jesus, in advance for your care and abundant good blessing in the Mighty name of Jesus!

Amen.

Sincerely, Julian Marie Walker

Author/Intercessor/Missionary

7. We The People Require Ethical Practices

Lord, I just remembered to add these to the list of prayers: Leaders in the synagogue, congress, lawyers, judges, teachers, council members, healthcare systems, insurance companies, real estate brokers, social security, court systems, banking systems, colleges and universities, tax collectors and providers, intellectual property thieves, residential property thieves, scammers on the web, and telephone collection agencies, credit card companies and social media companies. In your name — be Good and do good.

The prayer of a righteous person has great power to prevail.

Amen.

Dear reader!

Today, we take our faith to a higher level in Jesus Christ, regarding your family, health, and finances. Therefore, for every good and pure thing you believe in God for, you can join the Spiritual Agreement page. Write down your request and sign it!

____

____

Sign ____

We the body of believers ask God for supernatural miracles and manifestations according to his word John 14:14, " If ye shall ask anything in my name, I will do it". Thank you, Lord Jesus, in advance for your care and abundant good blessing in the Mighty name of Jesus!

Amen.

Sincerely, Julian Marie Walker

Author/Intercessor/Missionary

8. Surrender to The Will of God

Abba Father, help me this morning to transform my mind and thoughts so that I can release my burdens at your feet. May I never be like them. "And be not conformed to this world: but be ye transformed by the renewing of your mind, that ye may prove what is that good, and acceptable, and perfect, will of God" (Romans 12:2). Father, may I decrease and you increase in the mighty name of Jesus. It is written, Father God, that nothing is impossible for you, and I am holding on to your promise.

First and foremost, I am a child of God, and I give thanks for everything in Jesus' name. Nevertheless, today I place this petition concerning these cowardly, unbelieving, vile, sexually immoral, murderous, thieving, and scamming liars on earth into your hands. Our Father God does not hold back from giving them the same poison that they have injected.

Lord, shut down their evil copycat plans. Father, stop them so they cannot pour out any more wickedness and spread lies in this world. Lord, put a permanent cease to their mixed-up concoctions at their evil altars. Lord, bind up that jealous and envious spirit now and lay it to rest upon every wannabe and lookalike imposter. The Bible says in Ephesians 2:10, "For we are his workmanship, created in Christ Jesus unto good works, which God hath before ordained that we should walk in them." So be it.

Accordingly, as stated in the book of Revelation 21:8, "But the fearful, and unbelieving, and the abominable, and murderers, and whoremongers, and sorcerers, and idolaters, and all liars, shall have their part in the lake which burneth with fire and brimstone: which is the second death." Father, they are corrupt and have no regard for mankind. Father, I decree and declare with your power that for every dollar they scam and steal from me and mine, they will lose 470 times 70 of their own money.

Dear reader!

Today, we take our faith to a higher level in Jesus Christ, regarding your family, health, and finances. Therefore, for every good and pure thing you believe in God for, you can join the Spiritual Agreement page. Write down your request and sign it!

____

____

Sign ____

We the body of believers ask God for supernatural miracles and manifestations according to his word John 14:14, " If ye shall ask anything in my name, I will do it". Thank you, Lord Jesus, in advance for your care and abundant good blessing in the Mighty name of Jesus!

Amen.

Sincerely, Julian Marie Walker

Author/Intercessor/Missionary

9. Vengeance is The Lord's

They plot and steal bread from the sick, widows, and children for
a living. I am trusting that when you say, "Vengeance is Mine," says
the Lord, you will be faithful to your every word.
Father, you said, "Beloved, do not avenge yourselves, but rather give
place to wrath; for it is written, 'Vengeance is Mine, I will repay,'
says the Lord" (Romans 12:19). Father, may they reap what they sow.
May the houses and barns that they stole be burned down to the
ground, and may the wind blow away the ashes, never to form again.
May the lives they stole haunt them day and night forevermore. Put a
lock on their wealth and blessings. Father, if I overreach, forgive me. I
am a motherless child and a widow because of them. Father, I know
you will bring your judgment to this matter urgently today.

Father, I have cried and prayed for justice for so long that this day it
must be granted. I appeal to the Highest in heaven and earth for them
to pay for what they have done to my family. Father, you know I am
talking about money, titles, and deeds because those things are
rightfully ours. Some people forget the Bible verse: "For what shall it
profit a man if he shall gain the whole world and lose his soul?"
Remind them now, my God, before it is too late.

Accordingly stated in Mark 8:36, "For what shall it profit a
man, if he shall gain the whole world, and lose his soul?" Thank
you for setting me apart from these vile and wicked people. As stated
in 1 Peter 2:9, "But ye are a chosen generation, a royal priesthood, a
holy nation, a peculiar people; that ye should shew forth the praises of
Him who hath called you out of darkness into His marvelous light."

I thank you, LORD JESUS, over and over again for your grace, guidance, love, favor, protection, and provision. Lord, may their own malicious words and actions be exposed, causing them to fall by their own swords. Today I pray that they shall pay accordingly, as you, LORD, deem fit and justified, in the name of the Father, His Son Jesus Christ, and the Holy Spirit. May the will of God spearhead and lift this prayer to the throne of Heaven.

Amen.

Dear reader!

Today, we take our faith to a higher level in Jesus Christ, regarding your family, health, and finances. Therefore, for every good and pure thing you believe in God for, you can join the Spiritual Agreement page. Write down your request and sign it!

____

____

Sign ____

We the body of believers ask God for supernatural miracles and manifestations according to his word John 14:14, " If ye shall ask anything in my name, I will do it". Thank you, Lord Jesus, in advance for your care and abundant good blessing in the Mighty name of Jesus!

Amen.

Sincerely, Julian Marie Walker

Author/Intercessor/Missionary

10. Jehovah Raah The Lord is Shepherd.

Almighty God, who reigns over heaven and the earth. I want to personally thank you for being our most high father God and majestic creator of life on earth. Thank you for your abundant blessing and grace. Lord may it be pleasing to you as you minister to me this day through prayer and supplication. First and foremost, Jehovah Raah all praise unto you. Lord, you declare this how we pray, the Lord is my shepherd I shall not want.

"The LORD is my shepherd; I shall not want. He maketh me lie down in green pastures: he leadeth me beside the still waters. He restoreth my soul: he leadeth me in the paths of righteousness for his name's sake. Yea, though I walk through the valley of the shadow of death, I will fear no evil: for thou art with me; thy rod and thy staff they comfort me. Thou preparest a table before me in the presence of mine enemies: thou anointest my head with oil; my cup runneth over. Surely goodness and mercy shall follow me all the days of my life: and I will dwell in the house of the LORD forever" (Psalms 23:1-6).

In your word: Lord you declare and decree that surely goodness and mercy shall follow me all day of my life and I will dwell in the house of the Lord forever. Jehovah Raah, I thank you for my life, energy, family, friends favor, grace, good ethical and moral compass, Godly heritage, happiness, health, hope, joy, kindness, knowledge, love and longevity, integrity, power, provision, protection, peace, great wealth and riches, wisdom and understanding.

According to Father my great mighty God you declare in

Isaiah 7:9 "Of the increase of His government and peace, There

will be no end, Upon the throne of David and over His kingdom,

To order it and establish it with judgment and justice From that

time forward, even forever. The zeal of the LORD of hosts will

perform this. Jehovah Raah may your zeal power and grace

continue to bless me, from birth in the name of the Father, his

son Jesus Christ, and the Holy Spirit. Thank you, Lord, and

Thank you.

In Jesus' mighty name, I pray Amen.

Dear reader!

Today, we take our faith to a higher level in Jesus Christ, regarding your family, health, and finances. Therefore, for every good and pure thing you believe in God for, you can join the Spiritual Agreement page. Write down your request and sign it!

____

____

Sign ____

We the body of believers ask God for supernatural miracles and manifestations according to his word John 14:14, " If ye shall ask anything in my name, I will do it". Thank you, Lord Jesus, in advance for your care and abundant good blessing in the Mighty name of Jesus!

Amen.

Sincerely, Julian Marie Walker

Author/Intercessor/Missionary

11. Prayers Jehovah Shalom our Peace. Grace and mercy will be with us.

Heavenly Father, I thank you wholeheartedly for grace and mercy on this day. Therefore, we receive it according to 2 John 1:3: "Grace, mercy, and peace will be with us from God the Father and Jesus Christ, the Father's Son, in truth and love." Thank you for taking care of my family and loved ones. Lord, we thank you for giving us one day at a time. Lord, all we ask is that you give us the will, courage, and strength to do what we have to do always in the name of Jesus Christ.

Lord, help us to forgive each other as we seek your forgiveness in all things, knowingly or unknowingly. Lord, we know and trust that you are more than capable of taking care of all matters concerning your people. We know that with great confidence it is written: "Cast your burden on the LORD, and he will sustain you; he will never permit the righteous to be moved" (Psalm 55:22). Father, may you calm the storm and troubles concerning your righteous people. Peace be still, Jehovah Shalom; you are our peace.

Lord, according to Psalm 118:28–29, I declare: "You are my God, and I will praise you; you are my God, and I will exalt you. Give thanks to the LORD, for he is good; his love endures forever." Lord, keep us all safe in your care, and we give sincere thanks in advance to Jesus Christ our Lord.

Amen.

Dear reader!

Today, we take our faith to a higher level in Jesus Christ, regarding your family, health, and finances. Therefore, for every good and pure thing you believe in God for, you can join the Spiritual Agreement page. Write down your request and sign it!

____

____

Sign ____

We the body of believers ask God for supernatural miracles and manifestations according to his word John 14:14, " If ye shall ask anything in my name, I will do it". Thank you, Lord Jesus, in advance for your care and abundant good blessing in the Mighty name of Jesus!

Amen.

Sincerely, Julian Marie Walker

Author/Intercessor/Missionary

12. Jehovah Rapha God who heals

Heavenly Father, I thank you for this wonderful day, free
from all arrogant and curial people. Father, thank you for
sheltering me in your presence and keeping me safe from all
harm and hurt. Father, when you said my eyes would see them
fall to my right and fall to my left, but they cannot come near
me, I thank you Oh, Lord for powerful promises. Father, I
must thank you for your health and strength.

Father God you for strength my mind and my legs. Thank
you for being my Jehovah Rapha, the healer of my mind, soul,
and body. According to the Lord you said, Exodus 15:26 He
said, "If you listen carefully to the Lord your God and do what
is right in his eyes, if you pay attention to his commands and
keep all his decrees, I will not bring on you any of the diseases
I brought on the Egyptians, for I am the Lord, who heals you."
Father, there are no words to tell you how grateful I am,
thank you for being my covenant-keeping God. Lord if there is
anyone who needs this kind of healing tonight Lord be onto you
if they believe through the blood of Jesus Christ. Abba Father
my faith tells me that you are the Almighty God who heals and
can do it again and again. Lord have mercy and your children
as we cry out to you for all our needs.

Oh my God, "For ye have not received the spirit of bondage again, to fear; but ye have received the Spirit of adoption, whereby we cry, Abba, Father" (Romans 8:15). Father we are not helpless, but we know there is something only you can do and no one else. So, on behalf of your people, we pray for love, health, healing, forgiveness, and freedom. We are careful to request only what is of your will and thank you in advance for your hope, grace, guidance, mercy, protection, and provision in Jesus' mighty name we pray.

Amen.

Dear reader!

Today, we take our faith to a higher level in Jesus Christ, regarding your family, health, and finances. Therefore, for every good and pure thing you believe in God for, you can join the Spiritual Agreement page. Write down your request and sign it!

____

____

Sign ____

We the body of believers ask God for supernatural miracles and manifestations according to his word John 14:14, " If ye shall ask anything in my name, I will do it". Thank you, Lord Jesus, in advance for your care and abundant good blessing in the Mighty name of Jesus!

Amen.

Sincerely, Julian Marie Walker

13. Lord, We Trust in you.

Father Adonai, my Lord and protector who lives in my present, I come this day to offer thanks and praise. Lord, your people are grateful for what you continue to do in our lives. We are fully aware that you are a great and mighty God. Father, you are Jehovah Nissi, Lord our banner and rock. "The Rock, his work is perfect, for all his ways are justice. A God of faithfulness and without iniquity, just and upright is he" (Deuteronomy 32:4). Father God, as always, we give thanks for our children, family, and friends.

"Trust in the LORD with all your heart and lean not on your own understanding; in all your ways submit to him, and he will make your paths straight" (Proverbs 3:5–6). Father, you know them, and their names, and you know us by name, and we trust you are completely.

"Those who know your name trust in you, for you, LORD, have never forsaken those who seek you" (Psalms 9:10). Father, this day we just ask that whatever the needs are, they be met accordingly. Let your will be done. It is stated in James 4:15: "For that ye ought to say, If the Lord will, we shall live, and do this, or that."

Father, we know you are a faithful God, and you are faithful to keep your promises. We thank you in advance. May the Lord add a miraculous blessing to this prayer.

Amen.

Dear reader!

Today, we take our faith to a higher level in Jesus Christ, regarding your family, health, and finances. Therefore, for every good and pure thing you believe in God for, you can join the Spiritual Agreement page. Write down your request and sign it!

____

____

Sign ____

We the body of believers ask God for supernatural miracles and manifestations according to his word John 14:14, " If ye shall ask anything in my name, I will do it". Thank you, Lord Jesus, in advance for your care and abundant good blessing in the Mighty name of Jesus!

Amen.

Sincerely, Julian Marie Walker

14. Abba Father, we love with awe-filled reverence & obedience.

Abba Father, it's with great honor and gratitude that I come to you this day, giving my sincere thanks for all that you are and all that you do in our lives. Father, you are an amazing God, and we worship you in spirit and truth. The Bible says that if we love you with awe-filled reverence, obedience, and gratitude, then it is known by you, and we also are greatly loved by you. What a wonderful assurance. We thank you, Abba Father.

"But if anyone loves God [with awe-filled reverence, obedience, and gratitude], he is known by Him [as His very own and is greatly loved]" (1 Corinthians 8:3).

Heavenly Father, your children thank you for providing us with your best and seeing to it that we have all that we truly need. Thank you for peace in every season of our lives. The Good Book tells us that there is a time for every season under the heavens.

Lord, we are truly humble and grateful that you, Lord, make all the crooked paths straight, all the narrow roads wide, and put Good Samaritans on our road to always help us. "To everything there is a season, and a time to every purpose under heaven: a time to be born, and a time to die; a time to plant, and a time to pluck up that which is planted; a time to kill, and a time to heal; a time to break down, and a time to build up; a time to weep, and a time to laugh; a time to mourn, and a time to dance" (Ecclesiastes 3:1–4).

Father, you more than prove your love and favor for me each day. Lord, I exalt your name and lift you up. Thank you for lifting me above trials, pain, jealousy, and envy. Thank you for putting me on solid ground. Thank you, Lord. Lord, I am at the stage of my life where I choose to see and enjoy the beauty and blessings you have bestowed on me and around my life. Father, you are good to me all the time.

Thank you for giving me the wisdom to walk away from what you did not give me. Thank you for taking care of me, my children, family, and cherished ones. Thanks again, Lord, for giving me peace, according to John 14:27: "Peace I leave with you, my peace I give unto you: not as the world giveth, give I unto you. Let not your heart be troubled, neither let it be afraid." In Jesus' name, I pray. Selah.

Amen.

Dear reader!

Today, we take our faith to a higher level in Jesus Christ, regarding your family, health, and finances. Therefore, for every good and pure thing you believe in God for, you can join the Spiritual Agreement page. Write down your request and sign it!

____

____

Sign ____

We the body of believers ask God for supernatural miracles and manifestations according to his word John 14:14, " If ye shall ask anything in my name, I will do it". Thank you, Lord Jesus, in advance for your care and abundant good blessing in the Mighty name of Jesus!

Amen.

Sincerely, Julian Marie Walker

15. The Lord Opens The Portal of Heaven And Pours Out His Spirit

Heavenly Father here I come, in full powers of the Holy Spirit and intercede and appeal to the one and only Great and dreadful God of the universe. Accordingly, it is written "In the last days, God says, I will pour out my Spirit on all people. Your sons and daughters will prophesy, your young men will see visions, and your old men will dream dreams. Even on my servants, both men and women, I will pour out my Spirit in those days, and they will prophesy. I will show wonders in the heavens above and signs on the earth below, blood and fire and billows of smoke. The sun will be turned to darkness and the moon to blood before the coming of the great and glorious day of the Lord. And everyone who calls on the name of the Lord will be saved" (Acts 17-21).

Father before the Sunrise and Moonset may you turn over all their corrupt tables on them. Dear Lord, expose their evil and wickedness plots and put them to shame now. Fathers cut them down because they prey on our children, and they must stop at all costs. They used false voices, statements, airways, records, images, illness and bank accounts to hurt people for their selfish greed. Father these people twist the truth with lying tongues and falsify signatures and papers. Lord, may you pay them back 470 times 70.

May your blood deny the yoke of their spouse and firstborn for their cruel acts. I appeal to my great God that today they will fall on their arrogant sword, and may it pierce their own heart as they lose everything they have stolen from the poor.

Father, it is not with evil or malice intent I pray but for I pray for retribution, recompensating and restoration. May you Lord open all the portals of heaven to give way to the truth. In Jesus mighty name, I pray.

Amen.

Dear reader!

Today, we take our faith to a higher level in Jesus Christ, regarding your family, health, and finances. Therefore, for every good and pure thing you believe in God for, you can join the Spiritual Agreement page. Write down your request and sign it!

____

____

Sign ____

We the body of believers ask God for supernatural miracles and manifestations according to his word John 14:14, " If ye shall ask anything in my name, I will do it". Thank you, Lord Jesus, in advance for your care and abundant good blessing in the Mighty name of Jesus!

Amen.

Sincerely, Julian Marie Walker

16. The End has come for all false prophet and their evil worker

Dear Lord, how long will You allow these evil masked men and women to get away with what they have done? They have defiled, robbed, stolen, and lied. Bring truth to light and let justice prevail.

Lord, may every hidden thing be exposed and every evil plan be stopped. Remove their influence and scatter every work of deception, so that they can no longer harm or mislead others. Today we call upon the name of the Father, the Son Jesus Christ, and the Holy Spirit, because they were bold enough to carry out evil intentions. Father, bring justice for those who have been wronged.

The Bible states that when the righteous are in authority, the city rejoices. Lord, we ask for justice for Your people. A good man or woman should never be made a scapegoat for the actions of the wicked.

Vindicate Your people and set them free. Lord, bring healing, restoration, and peace to those who have suffered. In Jesus' name, I pray" "We are ambassadors for Christ, as though God were appealing through us; we beg you on behalf of Christ, be reconciled to God" (2 Corinthians 5:20).

Lord, You are able to bring happiness, health, and love. I know there is nothing You cannot do. Show up and show out, my Lord.

Lord, You are and always will be the great and mighty God of my grandparents and parents, and You are my God forever. "Therefore, He must reign until He has put all His enemies under His feet" (1 Corinthians 15:25).

Lord, I thank You in advance. My family thanks You. In Jesus'
powerful name I pray.
Amen and Amen.

Dear reader!

Today, we take our faith to a higher level in Jesus Christ, regarding your family, health, and finances. Therefore, for every good and pure thing you believe in God for, you can join the Spiritual Agreement page. Write down your request and sign it!

____

____

Sign ____

We the body of believers ask God for supernatural miracles and manifestations according to his word John 14:14, " If ye shall ask anything in my name, I will do it". Thank you, Lord Jesus, in advance for your care and abundant good blessing in the Mighty name of Jesus!

Amen.

Sincerely, Julian Marie Walker

17. Prayer God Grace

Our Father, whose heart is in heaven, gives us this day full of Your beauty and grace. We are truly grateful that You give us the most precious and priceless gift of life, health, love, and passion.

Therefore, we agree with 2 Corinthians 12:9: "But He said to me, 'My grace is sufficient for you, for My power is made perfect in weakness.' Therefore, I will boast all the more gladly in my weaknesses, so that the power of Christ may rest on me."

Father God, we are ever grateful for all provision and financial blessings You have set in place over our lives—things that no man can steal, but only You can release in Your timing.
Lord, once You decree a thing, it is so. Therefore, today we trust You completely, placing our hope in You for wealth, love, favor, and happiness, believing in increase in the mighty name of Jesus.

Lord, It is written: "I thank Christ Jesus our Lord, who has strengthened me, that He considered me faithful and appointed me to service" (1 Timothy 1:12).

My Lord, with Your mighty power, I decree and declare that anything that comes against me or my children's future must be brought under Your authority and removed from our path.

"And I will give unto thee the keys of the kingdom of heaven: and whatsoever thou shalt bind on earth shall be bound in heaven: and whatsoever thou shalt loose on earth shall be loosed in heaven" (Matthew 16:19).

Lord, we thank You in advance, in the name of the Father, the Son Jesus Christ, and the Holy Spirit.

Amen.

Dear reader!

Today, we take our faith to a higher level in Jesus Christ, regarding your family, health, and finances. Therefore, for every good and pure thing you believe in God for, you can join the Spiritual Agreement page. Write down your request and sign it!

____

____

Sign ____

We the body of believers ask God for supernatural miracles and manifestations according to his word John 14:14, " If ye shall ask anything in my name, I will do it". Thank you, Lord Jesus, in advance for your care and abundant good blessing in the Mighty name of Jesus!

Amen.

Sincerely, Julian Marie Walker

18. Jehovah Jireh our God Who provides.

Father God, I thank You for this day. Nevertheless, despite the forecasted weather of heavy rain, storms, and tornadoes, You are still good to Your people. Thank You for keeping us safe.

Therefore, all those who have been impacted by the weather, may God provide for them. Accordingly, it is written: "Jesus said to him, 'I am the way, and the truth, and the life. No one comes to the Father except through me'" (John 14:6).

We thank God for sound leadership and administration to assist the people in the community.

Father, we pray that all those who are in despair at this moment receive aid and experience a supernatural miracle—greater than what they have had before.

Lord, I thank You in advance on behalf of Your people. At this time, if You see fit, may You do for them what You do for me daily—turn weakness into strength and give them unstoppable and immovable faith.

Father, it is so wonderful to consider You the great Creator of all things. Thank You for making me wise and caring, but most of all for giving me faith that can never be taken away.

"No longer do I call you servants, for the servant does not know what his master is doing; but I have called you friends, for all that I have heard from My Father I have made known to you" (John 15:15).

Lord, thank You again for being my friend. Amen.

Dear reader!

Today, we take our faith to a higher level in Jesus Christ, regarding your family, health, and finances. Therefore, for every good and pure thing you believe in God for, you can join the Spiritual Agreement page. Write down your request and sign it!

____

____

Sign ____

We the body of believers ask God for supernatural miracles and manifestations according to his word John 14:14, " If ye shall ask anything in my name, I will do it". Thank you, Lord Jesus, in advance for your care and abundant good blessing in the Mighty name of Jesus!

Amen.

19. We Win in the name of Jesus Calling on the Lord to cancel out the Wicked and their Plans with the truth.

Abba Father according to your word it clearly states that whosoever that calls upon your name shall be saved: "For whosoever shall call upon the name of the Lord shall be saved" (Roman 10:13). Father, so today I call upon your name for your help. If it is your will, may you have mercy on their wicked soul. Father, whatever their plans and intentions are, blows it up in their wicked face and makes them shame publicly or for their crime put them in prison. May you keep them and their family in hell for a thousand generations.

Father don't hold back. May you give them everything they deserve. A life for a life, an eye for an eye. Father God, you said it in Leviticus 17-22, "Whoever takes a human life shall surely be put to death. Whoever takes an animal's life shall make it good, life for life. If anyone injures his neighbor, as he has done it shall be done to him, fracture for fracture, eye for eye, tooth for tooth; whatever injury he has given a person shall be given to him. Whoever kills an animal shall make it good, and whoever kills a person shall be put to death. You shall have the same rule for the sojourner and the native, for I am the LORD your God." Father, this is your law as of today they have no sponsor.

Their dreams are blown away like ashes. Father, if I am wrong, forgive me. But if I am right, burn them on earth and hell. This prayer is not for everyone, but those three wicked people. My dear, this is my condolence. May God expose your true identity and burn you to hell. "But the cowardly, the unbelieving, the vile, the murderers, the sexually immoral, those who practice magic arts, the idolaters, and all liars—they will be consigned to the fiery lake of burning Sulphur. This is the second death" (Revelation 21: 8).

God forgives so do I, but I will never forget you will pay. I promised in the name of the Father God his son Jesus Christ and the Holy Spirit. In Jesus's Matchless name. So be it.

Amen

Dear reader!

Today, we take our faith to a higher level in Jesus Christ, regarding your family, health, and finances. Therefore, for every good and pure thing you believe in God for, you can join the Spiritual Agreement page. Write down your request and sign it!

____

____

Sign ____

We the body of believers ask God for supernatural miracles and manifestations according to his word John 14:14, " If ye shall ask anything in my name, I will do it". Thank you, Lord Jesus, in advance for your care and abundant good blessing in the Mighty name of Jesus!

Amen.

20. When Jehovah Shammah Lord is [there]

LORD JESUS, I just want to thank You for waking me up this morning. Thank You for carrying me when I was too weak to walk. Thank You for providing for me and my offspring.

As long as I am alive, I will fight, and I will win because the Lord has declared it. I don't know what the devil is doing among these people, but Lord, I know You are in control of it all. I can assure them that I have victory in Jesus Christ's name.

Even when I didn't know, one day He revealed to me that no one in the world was like me, and He made it so. Amen. Therefore, for His purpose, I was created. Tell them they have failed the test of life—trying to rob, imitate, and even lie about others. My God is a witness in every city.

When Jehovah Shammah is there (Ezekiel 48:35), I will turn over every table in the sanctuary because of what they have done through partnership and unjust dealings. Jehovah Shammah means "THE LORD IS THERE."

"And Jesus went into the temple of God and cast out all of them that sold and bought in the temple, and overthrew the tables of the moneychangers, and the seats of them that sold doves, and said unto them, 'It is written, My house shall be called the house of prayer; but ye have made it a den of thieves'" (Matthew 21:12–13).

The Lord declares: "Rejoice with those who rejoice; mourn with those who mourn" (Romans 12:15). So, when I rejoiced with you, I wanted nothing from you, and when I mourned, I wanted nothing from you.

And by the way, you have it all wrong—you cry when the baby is born and rejoice when someone dies. Do not be selfish; they are with the Creator, and He holds the master key.

In Jesus' name, Amen.

Dear reader!

Today, we take our faith to a higher level in Jesus Christ, regarding your family, health, and finances. Therefore, for every good and pure thing you believe in God for, you can join the Spiritual Agreement page. Write down your request and sign it!

____

____

Sign ____

We the body of believers ask God for supernatural miracles and manifestations according to his word John 14:14, " If ye shall ask anything in my name, I will do it". Thank you, Lord Jesus, in advance for your care and abundant good blessing in the Mighty name of Jesus! Amen.

21. Fair Fight: Let all things be done decently and in order.

Heavenly Father, I call on You to forgive them for what they have done. Lord, we pray for peace and guidance. May You, Lord, protect us all in times of need.

Father, they have disguised themselves as good and decent people, robbing and stealing from the ordinary citizen. Lord, bring truth to light and let justice prevail.

Father, as for those who commit wrongdoing, You know what to do. They have missed the mark and have interfered with justice and humanity.

"Let all things be done decently and in order"
(1 Corinthians14:40).

Amen and Amen.

Dear reader!

Today, we take our faith to a higher level in Jesus Christ, regarding your family, health, and finances. Therefore, for every good and pure thing you believe in God for, you can join the Spiritual Agreement page. Write down your request and sign it!

____

____

Sign ____

We the body of believers ask God for supernatural miracles and manifestations according to his word John 14:14, " If ye shall ask anything in my name, I will do it". Thank you, Lord Jesus, in advance for your care and abundant good blessing in the Mighty name of Jesus!

Amen.

22. He cannot deny Himself

Our Father, whose heart is in Heaven, Father God, if ever there was a time we need You on earth, it is this day. The wicked are out of control. They have gloated and preyed on mothers and children, the weak and the loyal, for too long. Stop it this day and forevermore, in the name of Jesus.

Whatever they have stolen, let it be accounted for and never prosper in their hands. The next time they are about to lie, let truth prevail and expose deception. The next time they are about to commit fraud, let justice intervene and wrongdoing be brought to light.

Lord, You are witnessing that I am not lying, and I am holding on to Your promise. As for the faithful, bless them. According to God our Father, if we are faithless, "He remains faithful, for He cannot deny Himself" (2 Timothy 2:13).

I am trusting You to do what is right because You, the Creator, said, "God is not a man, that He should lie; neither the son of man, that He should repent: hath He said, and shall He not do it? Or hath, He spoken, and shall He not make it good?" (Numbers 23:19).

I am praying for healing, guidance, protection, and financial restoration on this day. I pray Psalm 91 over my life, my children, and grandchildren.

May the holy prayers of my mother continue to cover and protect me, and my children and grandchildren, and go before us in all things. In Jesus' name.
Amen.

Dear reader!

Today, we take our faith to a higher level in Jesus Christ, regarding your family, health, and finances. Therefore, for every good and pure thing you believe in God for, you can join the Spiritual Agreement page. Write down your request and sign it!

____

____

Sign ____

We the body of believers ask God for supernatural miracles and manifestations according to his word John 14:14, " If ye shall ask anything in my name, I will do it". Thank you, Lord Jesus, in advance for your care and abundant good blessing in the Mighty name of Jesus!

Amen.

23. I'm thankful to God for a grateful heart

God said it, He will surely do it. Well, Lord, You know I have been under the weather for the past thirty days. But the wisdom I have gained is priceless. I am grateful for good medical care and the kindness of family and real, professional, and even invisible friends.

Today was a good day. And no, I did not get the dream job, dream house, or dream husband yet, but what I have learned is priceless: faith, self-care, love, trust, and triumph over mediocrity, people, and problems.

We are all here on earth for different reasons. The key is to do the best job we can and take responsibility for what we do. Let those who lie or are dishonest be what they are—they will answer to You, Lord. I know justice does not forget an address. Let those who are kind and serving with fairness continue to be good, because justice does not forget an address.

According to the Bible, what does it profit a man to gain the whole world and lose his soul? I have lived my life mostly by the Book, with few regrets. I have loved and lost; I have fallen but I have gotten back up. I know You are always with me. I was blessed with a sweet soul, a beautiful heart, and yes—brains and beauty.

I am grateful that I have overcome bad days and now enjoy good days. My perspective has changed, and I no longer tolerate disrespect from people. I stand up for justice at all times. If I love you, I love you fully—there is no "if," "and" or "but" about it. I am committed to truth and integrity, and toxic relationships are now in Your hands, God.

I am grateful for my children and grandchildren, and I give thanks in advance for my expected great-grandchildren. This year at church, I remembered my mother's dying words: "Let it go…" and so, I am letting go.

There is too much beauty and goodness in God's grace to give it away to any human being in this life or any lifetime. My new motto is when they go low and nasty, I go higher and holy. In simple words: get thee behind me, Satan. By the power of the Almighty God who reigns in heaven and earth, you are finished.

I know that labor pain, toothache, and heart attack are painful—I never want to experience two of them again as long as I live. As for labor pain, I take the Holy Mary stance: "Be it unto me."

"And Mary said, 'Behold the handmaid of the Lord; be it unto me according to thy word. And the angel departed from her'" (Luke 1:38).

Forgive me, Lord. Thank You for giving me strong faith and keeping Your Word. "He gives strength to the weary and increases the power of the weak" (Isaiah 40:29). Amen and Selah.

P.S. Sincerely, thank You. "Behold, I will bring it health and healing; I will heal them and reveal to them an abundance of prosperity and security" (Jeremiah 33:6).

Amen.

Dear reader!

Today, we take our faith to a higher level in Jesus Christ, regarding your family, health, and finances. Therefore, for every good and pure thing you believe in God for, you can join the Spiritual Agreement page. Write down your request and sign it!

____

____

Sign ____

We the body of believers ask God for supernatural miracles and manifestations according to his word John 14:14, " If ye shall ask anything in my name, I will do it". Thank you, Lord Jesus, in advance for your care and abundant good blessing in the Mighty name of Jesus! Amen.

24. Jehovah Nassi The Lord is my Banner

Focus with wisdom to achieve wealth, wholeness, and happiness. There is not a day that I am not amazed by Your generosity and blessings. I thank You, Lord, for Your faithfulness and great grace. Thank You for always seeing the goodness in me. I feel truly blessed to live consistently and continuously in the grace of God. The truth is, in the past, what would have broken others has only made me stronger.

Jehovah my God, thank You for strong faith and the believer's anointing, and for reminding me that there is nothing my God cannot do when we pray. "But He said to me, 'My grace is sufficient for you, for My power is made perfect in weakness'" (2 Corinthians 12:9). Therefore, I will boast all the more gladly about my weaknesses, so that Christ's power may rest on me.

Lord, You are and will always be the everlasting Rock of all ages. I am truly thankful that You blessed me with a wise mother who taught me how to praise You through singing, worship, and prayer. Father, You know that on a day like today, when the gift of writing flows, I could go on telling You how amazing she was—but You already know. So, I simply say thank You for her, because the values she taught me are like oil and manna from heaven that never run out.

Maybe this is where I feel a little weak, but I would still give everything, just like the song says, to pray with her again or comb her hair. She said a woman's hair is her outer beauty, and her heart is her inner beauty. Forgive me, Lord, respectfully—my inner heart is showing for the world to see; I loved my mom deeply, despite it all.

I don't always understand God's plans, but I ask for courage to accept all the seasons of life. This one thing I am confident in is that my brothers and I were undeniably loved by her.

Dear reader!

Today, we take our faith to a higher level in Jesus Christ, regarding your family, health, and finances. Therefore, for every good and pure thing you believe in God for, you can join the Spiritual Agreement page. Write down your request and sign it!

____

____

Sign ____

We the body of believers ask God for supernatural miracles and manifestations according to his word John 14:14, " If ye shall ask anything in my name, I will do it". Thank you, Lord Jesus, in advance for your care and abundant good blessing in the Mighty name of Jesus!

Amen.

25. There is a season for everything

I know she is always with us in the spirit through prayer and supplication, making our requests always known to You. Father God, thank You for Your wisdom. It is still amazing to live in the blessing of God and in the pursuit of happiness. I am also blessed; greatness and worthiness are in my DNA.

Ecclesiastes states: "To everything there is a season, and a time to every purpose under the heaven: a time to be born, and a time to die; a time to plant, and a time to pluck up that which is planted; a time to kill, and a time to heal; a time to break down, and a time to build up; a time to weep, and a time to laugh; a time to mourn, and a time to dance; a time to cast away stones, and a time to gather stones together; a time to embrace, and a time to refrain from embracing; a time to get, and a time to lose; a time to keep, and a time to cast away; a time to rend, and a time to sew; a time to keep silence, and a time to speak; a time to love, and a time to hate; a time of war, and a time of peace" (Ecclesiastes 3:1–8).

In the name of the Father, His Son Jesus Christ, and the Holy Spirit, the Lord has given a blessing to His Word. Selah.

Amen.

Dear reader!

Today, we take our faith to a higher level in Jesus Christ, regarding your family, health, and finances. Therefore, for every good and pure thing you believe in God for, you can join the Spiritual Agreement page. Write down your request and sign it!

____

____

Sign ____

We the body of believers ask God for supernatural miracles and manifestations according to his word John 14:14, " If ye shall ask anything in my name, I will do it". Thank you, Lord Jesus, in advance for your care and abundant good blessing in the Mighty name of Jesus!

Amen.

26. Lord is my Banner Jehovah Nissi

Abba Father God, Son of David, I am here again giving my heartfelt praise, honor, and thanks for showing me an abundance of grace and favor. My Way Maker God, Lord, it is no secret the obstacles I have faced, including grief, yet I have survived. Oh my Lord, I am still here, faithfully holding on to Your every word and promise.

Lord, when they said You give the hardest battles to Your strongest soldiers, I never in a million light-years thought that would be me. Thus, as long as I live, Jehovah, You are my God. I will forever give thanks unto You, and I will answer when You call. I thank You for caring for me and holding my hand through the darkest days of sickness and confusion. Lord, thank You for my strong, wonderful, and grateful heart.

I thank You, Jehovah Rapha, for the supernatural miracles and for being my amazing healer. I thank You, Jehovah Jireh, for being my soul's and financial provider. I thank You, Jehovah Shalom, for being my Prince of Peace. Peace be still, Father.

Adonai, I thank You for being my great and mighty God. Love me and protect me. Lord, You heal my wounds and hear every cry. Lord, cast all my enemies to dust, never to rise again, so that Your purpose may be fulfilled.

Lord, Your Word states: "For this cause we also, since the day we heard it, do not cease to pray for you, and to desire that ye might be filled with the knowledge of His will in all wisdom and spiritual understanding" (Colossians 1:9–10).

Dear reader!

Today, we take our faith to a higher level in Jesus Christ, regarding your family, health, and finances. Therefore, for every good and pure thing you believe in God for, you can join the Spiritual Agreement page. Write down your request and sign it!

____

____

Sign ____

We the body of believers ask God for supernatural miracles and manifestations according to his word John 14:14, " If ye shall ask anything in my name, I will do it". Thank you, Lord Jesus, in advance for your care and abundant good blessing in the Mighty name of Jesus!

Amen.

27. Abundant Grace

Our Father, whose heart is in heaven, hallowed be Thy name. Thy kingdom come, Thy will be done on earth as it is in heaven. Give us this day our daily bread, and forgive us for our transgressions as we forgive others.

Father, I come before You with a full heart, giving You all the honor and the glory. I know, Lord, that You see my heart, and I promise that from this day forth I will strive to live a full and happy life through the grace I have received.

According to Romans 6:14, "For sin shall not have dominion over you: for ye are not under the law, but under grace." As it has been said, every day above the earth is a wonderful day. Thank You for being able and for being my greatest source of strength.

"And God is able to make all grace abound toward you; that ye, always having all sufficiency in all things, may abound to every good work" (2 Corinthians 9:8).

Thank You, Lord. In Jesus' name, Amen.

Dear reader!

Today, we take our faith to a higher level in Jesus Christ, regarding your family, health, and finances. Therefore, for every good and pure thing you believe in God for, you can join the Spiritual Agreement page. Write down your request and sign it!

____

____

Sign ____

We the body of believers ask God for supernatural miracles and manifestations according to his word John 14:14, " If ye shall ask anything in my name, I will do it". Thank you, Lord Jesus, in advance for your care and abundant good blessing in the Mighty name of Jesus! Amen.

28. Prayers for God to Intervene

Father God, I thank You for this day. We ask You, Lord, to bind up all demonic representations against Your Kingdom on earth. Remove all those who come to bring confusion and misunderstanding into our lives. Father, Your people must be free, and everything that was stolen from them must be returned a thousandfold.

The people cried out to Moses, and Moses prayed to Yahweh, and the fire died down, according to Numbers 11:2. Father, we ask that whoever rules and governs must do so with honesty and integrity.

Lord, if ever there was a time that Your people need You to intervene, it is right now. Make all lies stop today in the name of the Father, His Son, and the Holy Spirit. Father God, pull out the roots of wickedness and do according to Your will. Blow away every evil altar to dust. Dear God, continue to bless Your people of faith.

Help Your people to see the goodness in the land of the living. As Psalm 121 confirms and affirms:

"A Song of Degrees. I will lift up mine eyes unto the hills, from whence cometh my help. My help cometh from the Lord, which made heaven and earth. He will not suffer thy foot to be moved:

He that keepeth thee will not slumber. Behold, He that keepeth Israel shall neither slumber nor sleep. The Lord is thy keeper: the Lord is thy shade upon thy right hand."

Father, may we experience no lack and continue to praise and worship only You, our God. Thank You for hearing and granting my prayers, in Jesus' name.

Amen.

Dear reader!

Today, we take our faith to a higher level in Jesus Christ, regarding your family, health, and finances. Therefore, for every good and pure thing you believe in God for, you can join the Spiritual Agreement page. Write down your request and sign it!

____

____

Sign ____

We the body of believers ask God for supernatural miracles and manifestations according to his word John 14:14, " If ye shall ask anything in my name, I will do it". Thank you, Lord Jesus, in advance for your care and abundant good blessing in the Mighty name of Jesus! Amen.

29. Father, I Pray

Heavenly Father, You said our fight is not with flesh and blood, but against spiritual wickedness in high places. Father, this is Your Word according to Ephesians 6:12: "For we wrestle not against flesh and blood, but against principalities, against powers, against the rulers of the darkness of this world, against spiritual wickedness in high places."

So today, here I come with all the power of the Holy Spirit that You have invested in me, asking You to cast out evil from its illegal places. Remove it from our children, homes, churches, rental properties, courts, colleges, neighborhoods, police departments, politicians, healthcare facilities, leaders, and businesses.

"And I will give unto thee the keys of the kingdom of heaven: and whatsoever thou shalt bind on earth shall be bound in heaven: and whatsoever thou shalt loose on earth shall be loosed in heaven" (Matthew 16:19).

Bind them up, Lord, so they will never again be confused with the righteousness of God and decent people. May they no longer lie to or steal from us again. Purge evil from our lives, never to return, in the name of Jesus Christ.

Today, I declare and decree that everything that has been stolen will be restored. They will answer for all they have done in ways they could never imagine. This I leave in Your hands, Lord and Master.

In Jesus' mighty name, Amen.

30. Thank God for Supernatural Miracles

Father, in the name of Jesus, here I come filled with the power of the Holy Spirit, giving You thanks and praise for all You have done and are about to do for me and my family.

I thank You in advance for the supernatural miracles You perform for me and my children. This morning, we give thanks for love, guidance, and protection. We thank You for life, for constant day-to-day protection, grace, mercy, provision, healing, and joy.

Father, through faith, we believe that You, Lord, cast down any evil actions, persons, or hands that may dare to come against me or my children. We ask, Lord, that they never prosper, and that their wickedness be turned back upon them and publicly put to shame.

Father, on behalf of all my generations, we pray that You are, and will always be, the Supreme Almighty God, the ruler of the entire world. Lord, You are the Lion and the Lamb, the Rose of Sharon, the Alpha and Omega, and the only true God of Your people.

Father, I thank You for being my peace, protector, provider, healer, teacher, doctor, counselor, and the only true and righteous Judge in times of need. Lord God, we bless Your holy name. Father, this special prayer thanks You for guiding and protecting my children. Lord, I know You avenge the wicked who prey on Your children.

Lord, I thank You in Jesus' powerful and mighty name.

Amen.

Dear reader!

Today, we take our faith to a higher level in Jesus Christ, regarding your family, health, and finances. Therefore, for every good and pure thing you believe in God for, you can join the Spiritual Agreement page. Write down your request and sign it!

____

____

Sign ____

We the body of believers ask God for supernatural miracles and manifestations according to his word John 14:14, " If ye shall ask anything in my name, I will do it". Thank you, Lord Jesus, in advance for your care and abundant good blessing in the Mighty name of Jesus! Amen.

About the Author

Ms. Julian Marie Walker was born in Clarendon, Jamaica, West Indies. She lived in New York for over thirty years and attended the Metropolitan College of New York, where she earned a bachelor's degree in Professional Studies. She is also a graduate of Ohio Christian University, where she earned a master's degree in Business Administration.

She has been blessed by God as a mother of five children, five grandchildren, and one great-grandchild.

She attends and is a member of Tabernacle of Praise Church International in Georgia, where she serves as a deaconess. She is part of the intercessory prayer team and serves on the Global Mission Team. One of her passions is missionary work, both locally and internationally, including service in Belize, Haiti, and the Dominican Republic.

She has worked in food distribution, fellowship outreach, hospitals and medical clinics, and has visited the elderly and orphanages, as well as participated in building schools and churches. Ms. Walker has also volunteered with the Caribbean Association of Georgia as the first-ever female Sergeant-at-Arms.

Ms. Walker is a well-cultured, caring Christian with a godly heritage, committed to faith, moral ethics, and integrity, with a desire to further the growth of this organization through the advancement and empowerment of all people—not only in her community and regardless of nationality, but to all people.

Thus, she has a servant's heart and believes that great

servants make the greatest leaders in history. Her volunteering, work experience, and contributions reflect her character and achievements, grounded in her mother's greatest gift to her: the gift of service and prayer.

Acknowledgement

Jesus Christ is Lord!

Dedication

In memory of my mother, Victoria Marie Brown-Hyde; my father, Justin Walker; and my brother, Trooper Upton J. Walker, I give thanks.

I am thankful for the strength of God, my children, grandchildren—Camilla, Theisman, Ticori, Tennessee, and Jennifer—and my great-grandson, Kyree. I am also thankful for my nieces and nephews, as well as my former deans, teachers, and professors.

Thank you, Dr. Nelson, for helping me in my efforts to publish my books.

I pray for all missionaries around the world for continued protection and provision.